SEEK:
SCIENCE EXPLORATION, EXCITEMENT, AND KNOWLEDGE

Family Health and Science Festival

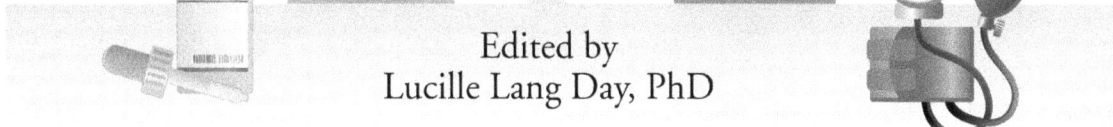

Edited by
Lucille Lang Day, PhD

I0202956

C·H·O·R·I
Children's Hospital Oakland Research Institute

SEPA
SCIENCE EDUCATION
PARTNERSHIP AWARD
Supported by the National Center for Research Resources, a part of the National Institutes of Health

Staff of Health and Biomedical Science for a Diverse Community

Co-Directors
Lucille Lang Day, PhD
Bertram H. Lubin, MD

Curriculum Developer and Program Coordinator
Laura McVittie Gray

Program Coordinators
Ava Holliday
Patricia Mielbeck
Sarah Reede

Curriculum Consultants
Leticia Márquez-Magaña, PhD
Marlene Wilson

Evaluators
Rita Gaber,
Kensington Research Group

Joseph Malloy, PhD,
Kensington Research Group

Presenters
High School Interns,
FACES for the Future,
Children's Hospital &
Research Center Oakland

College Interns,
Biology Scholars Program,
University of California at
Berkeley

Advisory Committee

Katharine Barrett
Charles Carlson
Mary Dean
Mary Frazier, RN
Marion Fredman
Charles Howarth
Caroline Kane, PhD

Do Kim
Janet King, PhD
Leslie Louie, PhD
Alexander Lucas, PhD
Tomás Magaña, MD
Leticia Márquez-Magaña, PhD
Gina Moreland

Laurie Schumacher, PhD
Barbara Stebbins, PhD
Kimberly Turner
Gordon Watson, PhD
Marlene Wilson

We are grateful to Tomás Magaña, MD, and Barbara Staggers, MD, co-directors of FACES for the Future, and to Caroline Kane, PhD, director of the Biology Scholars Program, for partnering with us to provide the many high school and college interns who have staffed the SEEK family health and science festivals.

Published by
Children's Hospital Oakland Research Institute
747 52nd Street, Oakland, CA 94609

Book designer: Debbie Dare
Copyright © 2010 by Children's Hospital Oakland Research Institute

ISBN: 978-0-9828252-1-1

This publication was made possible by a Science Education Partnership Award (SEPA), Grant Number R25RR020449, from the National Center for Research Resources (NCRR), a component of the National Institutes of Health (NIH). Its contents are solely the responsibility of the authors and do not necessarily represent the official views of NCRR or NIH. Additional support for this SEPA-funded project was provided by Grant Number UL1RR024131-01 from NCRR.

SEEK:
SCIENCE EXPLORATION, EXCITEMENT, AND KNOWLEDGE

Family Health and Science Festival

INTRODUCTION

Lucille Lang Day, PhD
Staff Scientist
Children's Hospital Oakland Research Institute
Former Director, Hall of Health

Bertram H. Lubin, MD
President and CEO
Children's Hospital & Research Center Oakland

The **SEEK** (**S**cience **E**xploration, **E**xcitement, and **K**nowledge) Family Health and Science Festival is a joint project of Children's Hospital Oakland Research Institute and Children's Hospital's Hall of Health Museum. Development of the festival was funded by a Science Education Partnership Award (SEPA), entitled Health and Biomedical Science for a Diverse Community, from the National Center for Research Resources at the National Institutes of Health.

The festival was designed to accompany the SEEK Curriculum in Health and Biomedical Science for diverse 4th and 5th grade students, but it can be presented independently at schools, museums, and other venues. The 19 SEEK Festival stations include hands-on activities related to the eight topic areas of the curriculum:

1. Nutrition: Balance and Imbalance
2. Traumatic Brain Injuries
3. Infectious Diseases
4. Environmental Toxics
5. Nutrition and Diabetes
6. Asthma and Lung Disease
7. Heart Disease
8. Genetics and Sickle Cell Anemia.

Upon arrival at the festival, each visitor receives a "passport," which has spaces for the names of the stations visited and brief statements of what was learned at each one. Upon completing each station, the visitor receives a sticker on the passport. After completing eight stations, the visitor receives a small prize, such as a forehead thermometer strip or a glow-in-the-dark eyeball. The festival stations can be completed in any order.

The festival has been presented at Children's Hospital Oakland, the Hall of Health, and many schools throughout the San Francisco Bay Area. Thousands of parents, teachers, and students have attended and provided feedback that has helped us to improve the stations. We are grateful to all of them. We are also grateful to the staff of the Lawrence Hall of Science and Explorit Science Center for sharing their expertise in the development of family science events.

Station 1: Organs of the Human Body

The Lesson

Your body is made up of specialized structures, called organs, that have specific functions. Some organs transport materials, while others help digest your food.

All body organs are important, and you can't live without them.

Equipment
Human torso model

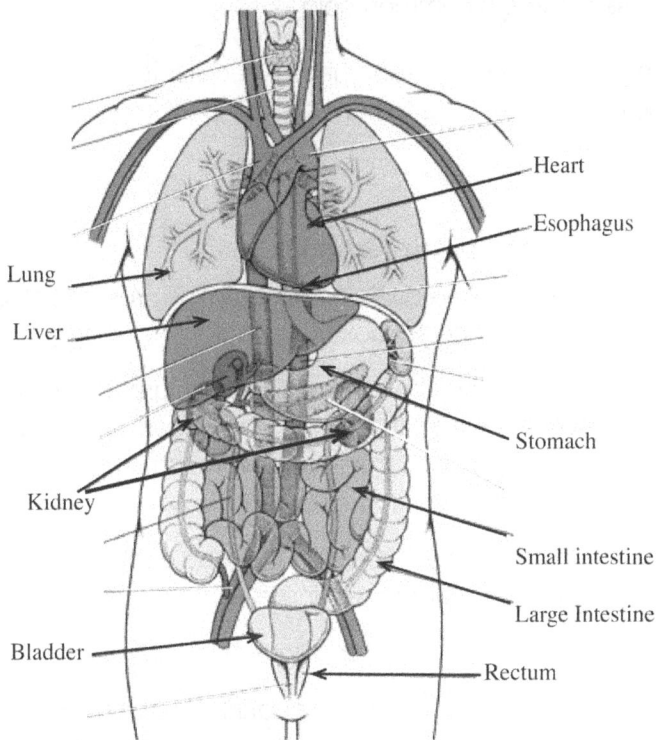

Labels on diagram: Heart, Esophagus, Lung, Liver, Stomach, Kidney, Small intestine, Large Intestine, Bladder, Rectum

Directions for the visitor

1. Say the name of each organ as you follow the organ diagram. Take out the organs in the following order: heart, lungs, liver, stomach, small and large intestines, kidneys, bladder, and brain.

2. Each organ plays an important role in the body:
   - **Heart:** pumps blood
   - **Lungs:** breathes in oxygen
   - **Liver:** cleans out poisons in the body
   - **Stomach:** mixes up and holds food
   - **Small and Large Intestines:** break down and absorb nutrients from food
   - **Kidneys:** remove waste from the blood and produce urine
   - **Bladder:** holds urine before you go to the bathroom
   - **Brain:** controls the body

3. Name all of the organs as you replace them in the correct places without using the diagram.

Station 2: Sugar and Fiber

The Lesson

If you eat sweet foods or drink sweet beverages only occasionally, your body can handle them. However, if you consume these foods in large quantities every day, your body will be in trouble.

HIGH sugar diets cause:

- Diabetes
- Mood swings
- Heart diease and high blood pressure (increased risk)
- Weight gain
- Decreased ability to fight off illnesses like the common cold

All of these health conditions limit your ability to play and have fun in life. If you want to fully enjoy your time, treat your body right and save the sweets for special treats.

Supplies

- ▸ "Nutrition Label" sheet
- ▸ "Low Sugar" sign
- ▸ "High Sugar" sign
- ▸ "Low Fiber" sign
- ▸ "High Fiber" sign
- ▸ 6 different cereal boxes
- ▸ 2 different soda bottles
- ▸ 1 milk carton
- ▸ 1 Gatorade bottle
- ▸ 1 Vitamin Water bottle
- ▸ 1 chocolate milk bottle

Directions for the visitor (Sugar)

1. Choose one type of food container to examine. You can choose either drink bottles or cereal boxes.

2. Guess which ones have the least and most sugar. Then line them up between the sign that says "Low Sugar" and the sign that says "High Sugar," according to how much sugar you think they contain.

3. Carefully examine the food labels on the food containers. Find the total amount of sugar per serving.

4. Rearrange the boxes to reflect the correct order.

5. What do you observe? Do you eat or drink products that are high in sugar? How often? How could sugary foods affect your health?

Station 2: Sugar and Fiber

The Lesson

A plant material found in food, fiber cannot be digested by the human body. However, it helps clean the digestive system. All fresh fruits and vegetables and whole grain breads and cereals contain fiber. Celery strings and orange strings are examples of fiber.

LOW fiber diets lead to:
- Higher risk for:
    - Heart disease
    - Diabetes
    - Diseases in your intestines
- Constipation (you have a hard time going to the bathroom)

Directions for the visitor (Fiber)

6. Guess which cereals have the least and most fiber. Is it more nutritious to have more fiber or less?

7. Between the sign that says "Low Fiber" and the sign that says "High Fiber," line up the containers from those you think have the least fiber to those you think have the most.

8. Carefully examine the food labels on the cereal boxes. Find the total amount of fiber per serving.

9. Rearrange the boxes to reflect the correct order

10. What do you observe? Do you eat cereals that are high in fiber? Why or why not?

Station 2: Sugar and Fiber

NUTRITION LABEL

The nutrition facts label gives us the energy and nutrient content of food items. In this food label from a cereal box, we can find the sugar and fiber content:

Sugars = 9 g

Dietary Fiber = 2 g

The sugar and fiber content of cereal allow us to determine how nutritious a cereal is. In general, a cereal higher in fiber and lower in sugar is more nutritious than one that is lower in fiber and higher in sugar.

Sugar and Fiber:

Sugar: Sugar is an energy source for our body, but eating an excess of sugar can lead to complications such as Type 2 Diabetes. This is why it is important to avoid foods that are high in sugar.

Fiber: It is important to consume fiber because fiber cleans our gastrointestinal tract and can help prevent cardiovascular disease. This is why foods higher in fiber content are considered more nutritious, although we can't digest fiber.

Nutrition Facts

Serving Size 3/4 cup (28g)

Servings Per Container about 14

Amount Per Serving	Honey Nut Cereal
Calories	110
Calories from Fat	15

	% Daily Value
Total Fat 1.5g	2%
Saturated Fat 0g	0%
Trans Fat 0g	
Polyunsaturated Fat 0.5g	
Monosaturated Fat 0.5g	
Cholesterol 0mg	0%
Sodium 190mg	8%
Potassium 115mg	3%
Total Carbohydrate 22g	7%
Dietary Fiber 2g	8%
Soluable Fiber less than 1g	
Sugars 9g	
Other Carbohydrate 11g	
Protein 3g	

Station 3: Energy Balance

The Lesson

- Energy balance means that you take in the same amount of energy that you use. You take in energy when you eat food, and you spend energy as you live, breathe and do physical activities.

- If the food side of the balance is heavier, then you are taking in more energy than that you're using. Over time, this excess energy will be stored as fat, and you will gain weight.

- If the activity side of the balance is heavier, then you are using more energy than you are taking in. Over time, you will lose weight.

- If both sizes of the balance are equal in weight, then you have an energy balance. This is a healthy way to live.

Supplies

- Mini poker chips (pennies can be used instead)

- Pictures of food with the calories given on back

- Pictures of activities with calories burned per hour given on back

- Plastic balance with two pans

Directions for the visitor

1. Do you think you use all of the calories you eat in one day?

2. Choose the foods that you would typically eat in one day. For every 50 calories eaten, place one poker chip in one side of the balance.

3. Choose the activities that you would do in one day. For every 50 calories used while exercising, place a poker chip on the other side of the balance. To this side, you can also add 24 chips for the 1,200 calories used for breathing, heartbeat, digestion, etc.

4. Which side of the balance is heavier? What would you have to add or subtract to make the two sides even?

Station 4: Serving Sizes

The Lesson

A serving size is the recommended amount of a certain food that one person should eat at one meal. There are different serving sizes for different types of food. Serving sizes can be easily estimated using household items:

Type of Food	Serving Size
Fruit, cereal, or pasta	1 tennis ball
Vegetable	1 lightbulb
Meat	1 deck of playing cards
Fish	1 checkbook
Butter	1 die
Cheese	3 dominos
Dinner roll	1 yo-yo
Peanut butter	1 film canister
Potato	1 computer mouse

Supplies
- Plastic food items or photos: broccoli, pasta, orange, hamburger patty, fish, cheese, peanut butter, cereal, dinner roll, potato, butter

- Household items: 60-W lightbulb, deck of playing cards, checkbook, die, 3 dominos, yo-yo, film canister, tennis ball, computer mouse

Directions for the visitor

1. Look at the pictures and plastic food items on the table.

2. For each food item, guess which household item represents the appropriate size for one serving. Put the food items together with the items that represent the appropriate serving sizes.

3. Look at the table of foods and serving sizes.

4. How many serving sizes did you guess correctly?

Station 5: The Amazing Broncholis

The Lesson

- Asthma is a disease that affects the lungs and respiratory system. When someone with asthma comes in contact with certain things, called "triggers," the tissues in their lungs swell, tighten, and produce mucus. They cough and wheeze. "Triggers" can include dust, pollen, animal hair, fumes, mold, exercise, cold air, fragrances, and cigarette smoke.

- Five percent of American adults and 8 percent of children have asthma.

- People with asthma use special medicines called controllers every day to prevent asthma attacks. They use other medications called relievers when they have an attack.

Supplies
- ▶ 5 LeapFrog Quantum Pads
- ▶ 5 LeapFrog Headphones
- ▶ 5 LeapFrog *Meet the Amazing Broncholis!* books
- ▶ 5 LeapFrog *Meet the Amazing Broncholis!* cartridges

Directions for the visitor

1. Put on the headphones and press the "On" switch at the right side of the Quantum Pad.

2. Turn to the first page of the story and press the green "Go" button with the pen.

3. To start each new page, press the green "Go" button on that page.

4. What did you learn about asthma? What causes an asthma attack, and what can be done to help patients?

Station 6: Test Your Lungs!

The Lesson

Peak flow meters are tools used by healthcare professionals and patients with asthma to measure the health of the lungs and respiratory system. Peak flow meters measure how fast you can force air out of your lungs. People with asthma or other respiratory diseases tend to have lower readings. However, do not be alarmed if you get a low reading. There is a range of normal readings for every age group.

Supplies
▸ Peak flow chart for children
▸ Peak flow chart for adults
▸ 4 peak flow meters
▸ Bag of disposable cardboard mouthpieces for peak flow meters
▸ 2 six-foot measuring tapes
▸ Asthma inhaler

Directions for the visitor

1. Attach a disposable cardboard mouthpiece to a peak flow meter.

2. Stand up straight and hold the peak flow meter around the mouthpiece with one hand.

3. Move the red indicator tab down to the bottom of the number scale. Make sure that your hand is not blocking the opening at the back of the peak flow meter.

4. Take a deep breath and forcefully blow into the peak flow meter in one long exhale.

5. Read the number to which the indicator tab rises and compare your result to the chart of average readings for your age group and height.

6. Do you think your reading would higher or lower if you were taller? Why?

Normal Predicted Average Peak Expiratory Flow for Children (in liters/minute)

Height (inches)	Peak Flow	Height (inches)	Peak Flow	Height (inches)	Peak Flow
43	147	51	254	59	360
44	160	52	267	60	373
45	173	53	280	61	387
46	187	54	293	62	400
47	200	55	307	63	413
48	214	56	320	64	427
49	227	57	334	65	440
50	240	58	347	66	454

Women

Age	Height				
	55"	60"	65"	70"	75"
20	390	423	460	496	529
25	385	418	454	490	523
30	380	413	448	483	516
35	375	408	442	476	509
40	370	402	436	470	502
45	365	397	430	464	495
50	360	391	424	457	488
55	355	386	418	451	482
60	350	380	415	445	475
65	345	375	406	439	468
70	340	369	400	432	461

Peak flow values in liters/minute

Men

Age	Height				
	60"	65"	70"	75"	80"
20	554	602	649	693	740
25	543	590	636	679	725
30	532	577	622	664	710
35	521	565	609	651	695
40	509	552	596	636	680
45	498	540	583	622	665
50	486	527	569	607	649
55	475	515	556	593	634
60	463	502	542	578	618
65	452	490	529	564	603
70	440	477	515	550	587

Peak flow values in liters/minute

Station 7: Pig Lungs

The Lesson

The respiratory system is made up of lung tissue and air passages. The air passages include the mouth, nose, throat, trachea, bronchi, and bronchioles. These passages lead to lung tissue, which has thousands of tiny air sacs called alveoli. When you breathe in, air travels through the air passages to the alveoli, where oxygen is received. As you breathe out, the lungs deflate, sending carbon dioxide back out your mouth and nose.

Supplies
- Pig lung display, including stand
- Box of latex gloves
- Lung diagram

Directions for the visitor

1. Slowly press the foot pump so that the pig lung inflates.

2. Release the foot pump so that the pig lung deflates.

3. What do you notice?

4. Look at the lung diagram. What parts of the respiratory system can you identify in the pig lung display? What are they doing?

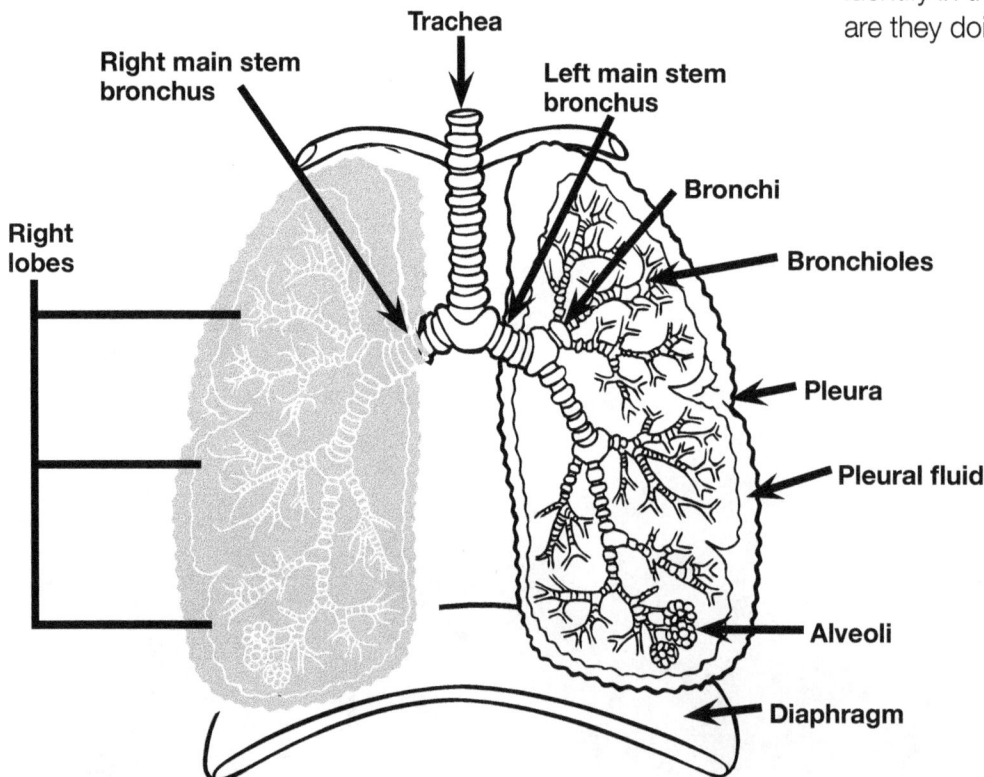

Trachea

Right main stem bronchus

Left main stem bronchus

Bronchi

Bronchioles

Right lobes

Pleura

Pleural fluid

Alveoli

Diaphragm

Station 8: Diagnosing Diabetes

The Lesson

- The test strip dipped in normal urine should be blue or green. If the test strip from the patient turns dark brown, then the patient has diabetes.
- Diabetes is a disease where a person has excess sugar in his or her blood. It can lead to serious health problems, including blindness, skin rashes, poor circulation, and even amputation (where an arm or leg must be removed).
- Diabetes can be passed down in a family. People can also develop it later in life. Excessive weight gain and poor health habits make development of diabetes more likely.

Supplies

► Bottle of Diastix Reagent Strips for Urinalysis

► 2 small urine bottles (low and high dextrose, labeled, respectively, "Normal" and "Patient")

► Color key for urine test

► Copies of the patient profile

► Make fake urine as follows (one drop of yellow food coloring may be added to each liter; pour into small bottles for activity):

- Mix 1 liter of water with 2.5 mg of dextrose, label "Normal"

- Mix 1 liter of water with 15 mg of dextrose, label "Patient"

Directions for the visitor

1. Take a urine test strip. Dip it into the urine labeled "Normal."

2. Wait 20 seconds for the strip to change color.

3. Compare the final color to the urine chart and determine the blood sugar level.

4. Read the patient profile. Then take another urine test strip and dip it into the urine labeled "Patient."

5. Wait 20 seconds for the strip to change color.

6. Compare the final color to the urine chart and determine the blood sugar level of the patient. Is the patient's blood sugar high, low, or normal?

Station 8: Diagnosing Diabetes

ANDY

Andy went to visit the doctor because he was not feeling well. He told the doctor he had the following symptoms: increased thirst, increased urination, hunger, being tired, and weight loss. The doctor thought these symptoms might indicate that Andy had diabetes.

The doctor decided to perform a test to see if Andy really had diabetes. To perform the test, he gave Andy a glass of sugar water to drink. Four hours later, the doctor measured the level of sugar in Andy's urine. If Andy has diabetes, the test will show that he has a high level of sugar in his urine. If he does not have diabetes, the test will show that he has a normal level of sugar in his urine.

Perform the test yourself to see if Andy has diabetes.

Is the sugar level in Andy's urine high or normal? (Circle your answer)

High   Normal

Does Andy have diabetes? (Circle your answer)

Yes   No

Children's Hospital Oakland Research Institute

Station 9: Your Brain

The Lesson

Left-brained people:

- Enjoy math
- Like to be organized and make lists
- Remember people by their names, not their faces
- Can easily memorize facts
- Understand literal meaning

Right-brained people:

- Are creative, enjoy writing or art
- Are often disorganized
- Remember people by their faces
- Are spatially aware, talk with their hands
- Are "big picture" oriented

Supplies

- ▸ Brain model
- ▸ Brain diagram
- ▸ Pencils
- ▸ Copies of quiz, Are you right- or left brained?
- ▸ 4 rulers
- ▸ Full-length, half-length, and third-length pipe cleaners, in three different colors

---

Directions for the visitor - Brain Model

1. Look at the brain model.

2. Compare the model to the brain diagram.
   How many parts of the brain can you identify?

Directions for the visitor - Right/Left Brain Quiz

1. Take the test and answer the questions.

2. Count up the number of times you answered YES.

3. If you have more "YES" than "NO" answers, you are right-brained.

4. If you have more "NO" than "YES" answers, you are left-brained.

5. If you have an even number of "YES" and "NO" answers, then you use both sides of your brain equally.

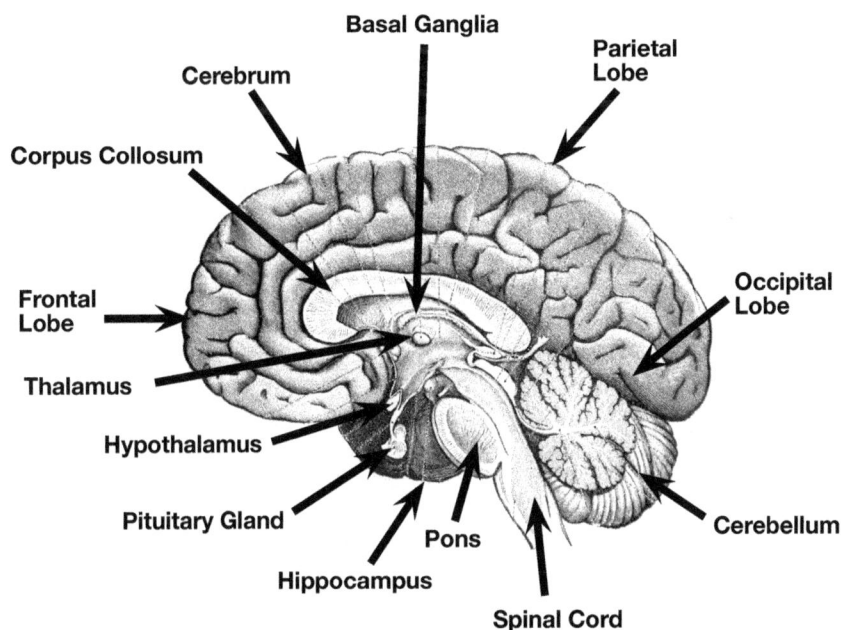

Brain diagram labels: Basal Ganglia, Cerebrum, Corpus Collosum, Parietal Lobe, Frontal Lobe, Thalamus, Hypothalamus, Pituitary Gland, Hippocampus, Pons, Spinal Cord, Occipital Lobe, Cerebellum

Station 9: Your Brain

ARE YOU LEFT- OR RIGHT-BRAINED?

YES NO 1. Do you enjoy creative writing more than math?

YES NO 2. Do you keep your desk cluttered?

YES NO 3. Do you remember people better by their faces instead of their names?

YES NO 4. Do you use a lot of hand motions when you talk?

YES NO 5. Can you tell about how much time has passed without a watch?

YES NO 6. Do you like drawing better than writing?

YES NO 7. Do you put your things in different places after you use them instead of always putting them away in the same place?

YES NO 8. Do you like tests where you must write your own answer better than multiple-choice tests?

Station 9: Your Brain

The Lesson | Neurons are specialized cells that send and receive signals in the brain and all through the body. You have billions and billions of these cells.

Directions for the visitor - Pipe Cleaner Neurons

1. Take one long pipe cleaner and roll one end into a ball. This ball represents the cell, the main part of the nerve cell, or neuron. The tail end is called the axon.

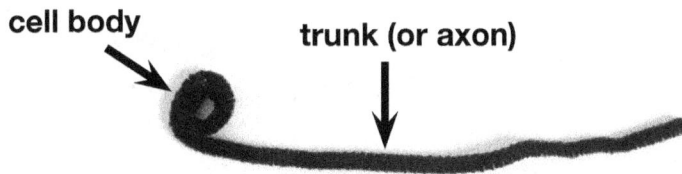

cell body   **trunk (or axon)**

2. Take 3 short pieces of pipe cleaner and twist them through the cell body so that they stick out like branches. These parts are called the dendrites.

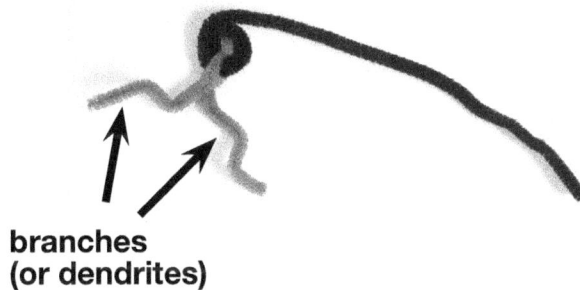

**branches
(or dendrites)**

3. Take a medium-length pipe cleaner and wrap it around the trunk or axon. This sheath acts as insulation, just like the plastic tubing found around electric wires.

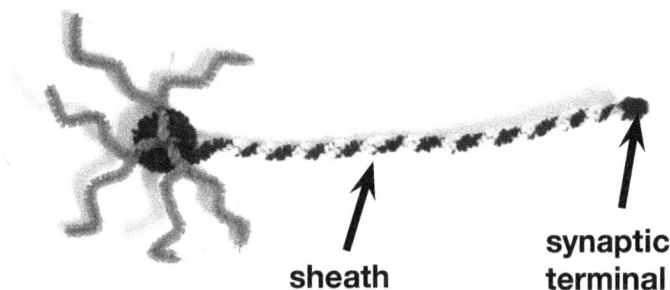

sheath   **synaptic terminal**

YOU JUST made a model OF a NeURON!

Children's Hospital Oakland Research Institute

Station 9: Your Brain

The Lesson | Reaction time is the speed at which your brain reacts to something. When you see the ruler drop, your brain sends a signal to your fingers and then your fingers grab the ruler.

Directions for the visitor - Reaction Time: Ruler Drop Test

1. Find a volunteer to hold a ruler dangling from the end with the high numbers.

2. Hold out your thumb and index finger just below the bottom end of the ruler ready to catch it.

3. When the volunteer drops the ruler without warning, try to catch it as fast as you can.

4. Look at the mark where your fingers caught the ruler and record the measurement. Compare it to the chart below. The lower the number you got, the faster your reaction time will be.

5. Try the test again to see if you can break your previous record.

Distance on Ruler	Reaction Time
2 in	0.10 sec
3 in	0.12 sec
4 in	0.14 sec
5 in	0.15 sec
6 in	0.17 sec
7 in	0.185 sec
8 in	0.20 sec
9 in	0.215 sec
10 in	0.23 sec
11 in	0.24 sec

Station 10: Heart Map

The Lesson

The circulatory system is group of organs and tissues that work together to transport nutrients and materials around the body. The central organ of the circulatory system is the heart, which pumps blood around the body through tubes called blood vessels. In the process, oxygen from the lungs is delivered to the cells, and a waste product called carbon dioxide is taken to the lungs.

Supplies

- ▶ 1 8-ft x 12-ft heart map with latex paint on canvas

- ▶ 1 set of large heart anatomy labels:
  - left atrium (1)
  - left ventricle (1)
  - aorta (1)
  - aorta valve (4)
  - arteries (2)
  - capillaries (2)
  - veins (2)
  - right atrium (1)
  - right ventricle (1)

- ▶ 5 red balls to represent O_2

- ▶ 5 blue balls to represent CO_2

- ▶ 1 Circulatory System Diagram

Directions for the visitor - Label the Heart

1. Study the Circulatory System Diagram alone or in a group.

2. Take off your shoes and select a label.

3. Walk around the heart and place the label in the correct place.

4. Each member of a group should repeat steps 2 and 3 with the other labels.

Directions for the visitor - Be a Red Blood Cell

1. Take off your shoes. Go to the lung tissue and pick up an oxygen ball.

2. Walk through the circulatory system to the capillaries of the body tissue.

3. Exchange oxygen for carbon dioxide.

4. Return through the circulatory system to the lungs.

5. Exchange carbon dioxide for oxygen.

6. Try it again and see how quickly you can complete the course.

Circulatory System Diagram

CO_2 is exchanged for O_2 in the capillaries of the lungs

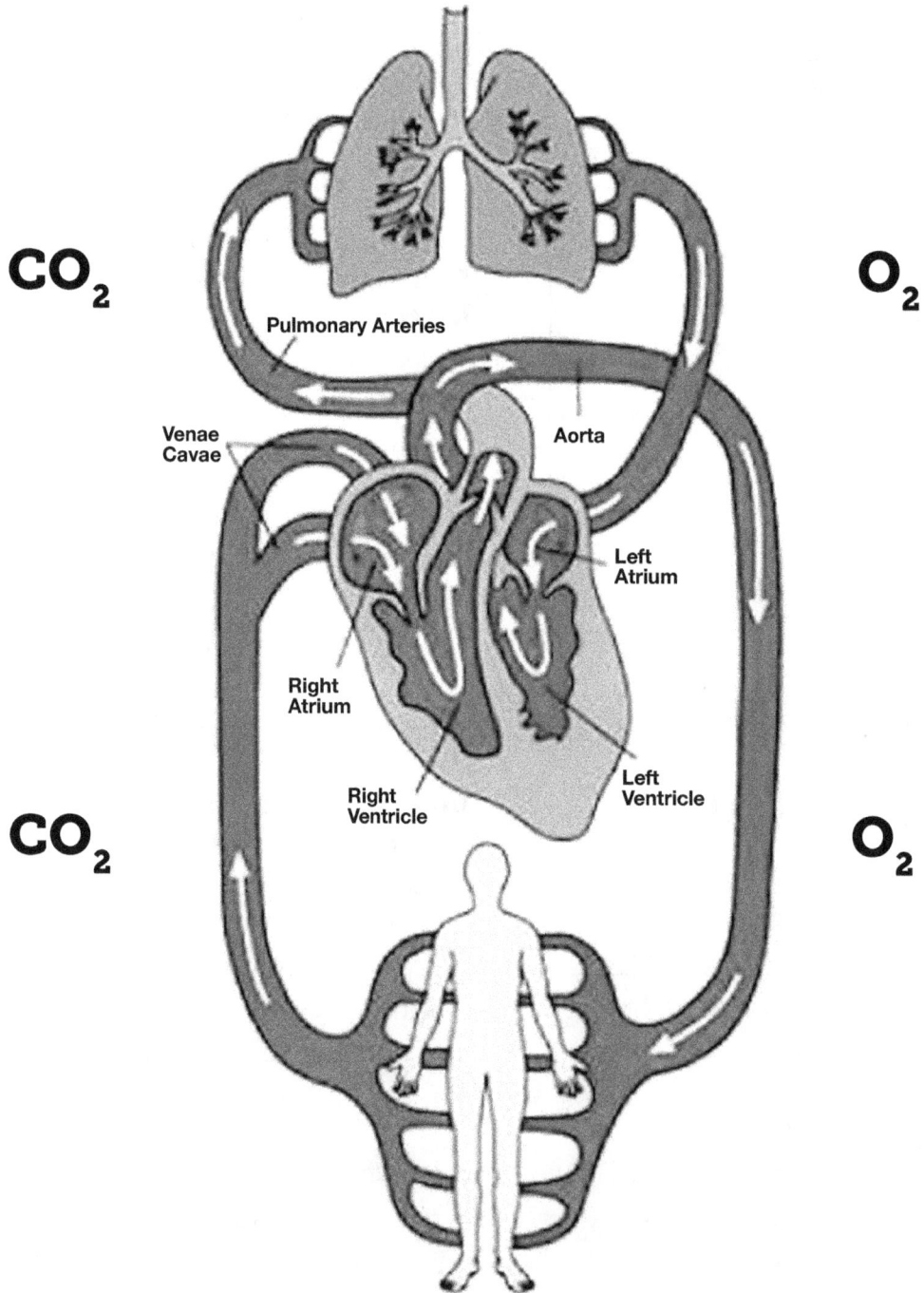

CO$_2$

O$_2$

Pulmonary Arteries

Venae Cavae

Aorta

Right Atrium

Left Atrium

CO$_2$

O$_2$

Right Ventricle

Left Ventricle

O_2 is exchanged for CO_2 in the capillaries of the body

Station 11: Blood Pressure

The Lesson

High blood pressure, or hypertension, can lead to serious health conditions such as heart attacks and strokes. You can prevent hypertension by eating a balanced diet and exercising regularly.

Supplies
▶ 2 child blood pressure cuffs

▶ 2 adult blood pressure cuffs

▶ 4 stethoscopes

▶ Blood pressure information sheet

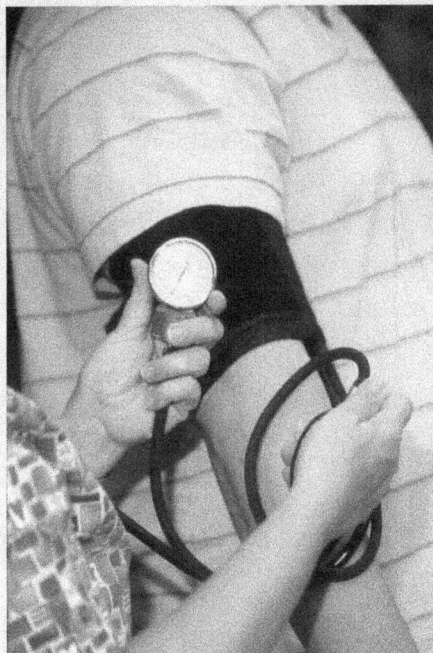

Directions for the visitor -
Using a Manual Blood Pressure Monitor

1. Place the cuff on your partners arm just above the elbow with the air tubes coming out over the inside of your elbow, where there is a large artery.

2. Place the round end of the stethoscope over the artery and just under the cuff. Place the other two ends in your ears.

3. Hold the bulb of the pump in your hand. Make sure that the knob is turned all the way to the right.

4. Pump the gauge up to about 140 for a child or 200 for an adult.

5. Slowly release pressure by turning the knob to the left. Stop when you hear the heartbeat and record the number. This is the systolic pressure.

6. Continue to release pressure by turning the knob to the left. Stop when you can't hear the heartbeat anymore. Record this number as the diastolic pressure.

7. Don't worry if your pressure isn't within the normal range. Taking blood pressure requires training and practice.

Normal Blood Pressure	
Average infant	70/40
Average child	100/60
Average teen or adult	120/80

Station 11: Blood Pressure

BLOOD PRESSURE INFORMATION

	The last time you went in for a check-up, did the nurse put a band around your arm that inflated like a balloon?	YES NO	Did your arm feel squeezed?	YES NO

The nurse was measuring your blood pressure with a blood pressure monitor. This test shows how hard your heart is pumping to move blood through your body. Blood pressure can be too high or too low, but yours is probably just right.

Blood pressure is the force of blood pressing against the walls of your blood vessels. It is measured using two numbers. The first measurement is the force of the blood when the heart squeezes. This is called systolic blood pressure. The second number measures the force of the blood when the heart relaxes. This is called diastolic blood pressure. Your blood pressure is written with the first number on top and the second number on the bottom.

If your blood pressure reading is different from the norm, don't worry. It takes practice and training to get accurate results with blood pressure monitors. Do have your blood pressure checked regularly by a healthcare professional. If your doctor thinks your blood pressure is too high, you should pay attention. High blood pressure, or hypertension, can lead to serious health conditions such as heart attacks and strokes. You can prevent hypertension by eating a balanced diet and exercising regularly.

Systolic: When heart is contracting

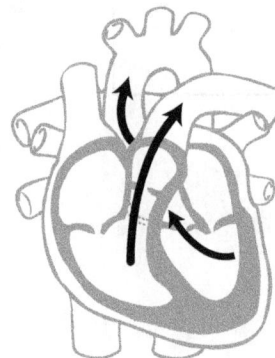

Diastolic: When heart is at rest

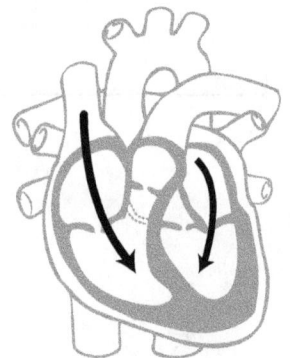

Normal Blood Pressure	
Average infant	70/40
Average child	100/60
Average teen or adult	120/80

Station 12: Your Traits and Talents

The Lesson

Traits include characteristics such as eye color, ear shape, height, and nose size. You have some characteristics that you inherited at birth from your parents, through the genetic code in your DNA. Inherited traits include things like your hair color, chin shape, and presence (or absence) of dimples. You get other traits during the course of your lifetime. Scars, tattoos, colored hair, and pierced ears are all examples of traits that you acquire.

Supplies

► Copies of "An Inventory of My Traits and Talents"

► Pencils

► Answer key

► "Genetic and Acquired Traits" information sheet

Directions for the visitor - Label the Heart

1. Complete "An Inventory of My Traits and Talents."

2. Check the traits that you think are inherited.

3. Look at the answer key to see how many you got right!

Station 12:
An Inventory of My Traits and Talents
ANSWER KEY

Note: Some traits, such as ability to run fast or play a musical instrument are not inherited, but are influenced by your genes. For example, you can run faster if you have long legs, and your ability to play a musical instrument may be affected by genes for long fingers or perfect pitch.

Feature	Yes	No	Check if you think it's genetically inherited
Are you right handed?			Yes
Can you play a musical instrument?			No
Do you have long legs?			Yes
Do you clasp your hands with your right thumb on top?			Yes
Can you run fast?			No
Do you have dimples?			Yes
Can you roll your tongue into a U?			Yes
Can you hold your breath for a long time?			No
Are you good at video games?			No
Do your earlobes attach at the ends of your ears?			Yes
Are you good at basketball?			No
Do you like chocolate?			No
Do you have a cleft chin?			Yes

Station 12: An Inventory of

MY TRAITS AND TALENTS

1. Answer each question with a yes or no.

2. Then vote if you think the feature is an inherited trait (something that got passed to you from your parents) or just about you.

Feature	Yes	No	Check if you think it's genetically inherited
Are you right handed?			
Can you play a musical instrument?			
Do you have long legs?			
Do you clasp your hands with your right thumb on top?			
Can you run fast?			
Do you have dimples?			
Can you roll your tongue into a U?			
Can you hold your breath for a long time?			
Are you good at video games?			
Do your earlobes attach at the ends of your ears?			
Are you good at basketball?			
Do you like chocolate?			
Do you have a cleft chin?			

Station 12: Genetic and Acquired Traits

Why do you LOOK the way you do?

Your characteristics are called TRaiTS.
Maybe you're tall with black hair or short with red hair and freckles.

Some of these traits are a result of things that you learned, experiences you had, or changes you decided to make:

You might have a scar from an accident or a sunburn from spending too much time in the sun. You might have orange hair because you dyed it. These are all acquired traits: you weren't born that way.

Other traits, called genetic traits, are ones you were born with. These are inherited through genes that were passed down to your from your parents.

Inherited Traits	Acquired traits
Natural eye color	Scars from accidents
Earlobe shape	Dyed hair color
Nose shape	Clothes you are wearing
Eyesight	Tattoos
Dimples	Glasses

Then, there are traits that are a combination of genetically inherited and acquired traits.

For example, you may inherit genes for your height from your parents, but your diet affects how tall you grow. You may inherit genes that predispose you to heart disease but never develop it if you take good care of your health.

geNes

- Genes are like recipes or blueprints for your body. They are instructions for how your body is made and how it functions.

- Genes are found in the nucleus of most of your body cells. Some cells lose the nucleus and genes when then mature.

Station 13: Potato Head Genetics

The Lesson

We have two copies of each of our genes, one from our mother and one from our father. These genes can differ slightly from each other. Some forms of a gene are called "dominant" and some forms are called "recessive":

Dominant: The dominant form of a gene is expressed even when an individual only has one copy of it. That is, of the two genes he or she has for a particular trait, one copy is dominant and one copy is recessive.

Recessive: The recessive form of a gene is expressed only when an individual has two copies of it.

Supplies

▶ Station 13 "Instructions for the Visitor"

▶ 6 Mr. Potato Head toys

▶ 12 coins

▶ 6 boxes of colored pencils or crayons

▶ Copies of Mr. Potato Head Worksheet

▶ Copies of Dominant and Recessive Trait Survey

Station 13: Potato Head Genetics

TRAIT INHERITANCE

Genetic Traits for Potato Heads

Trait	Dominant	Recessive
Hair	Bald	Orange
Ears	Round	Flat and invisible
Nose	Red	Orange
Mouth	Big teeth	No teeth, only tongue
Arms	Yellow	White

Coin Toss

1. Decide on one trait. Read the dominant and recessive versions of the trait.
2. Flip two coins.
3. Determine which trait wins:

If you get two heads...

...then the dominant trait wins.

If you get two tails...

...then the recessive trait wins.

If you get a heads and a tails...

...then the dominant trait wins.

4. Place the winning trait on your Potato Head child.

5. Repeat steps 1 to 4 for the remaining traits.

Station 13: Potato Head Genetics

POTATO HEAD KID

Draw your Potato Head kid, and draw an arrow to traits inherited through genes.

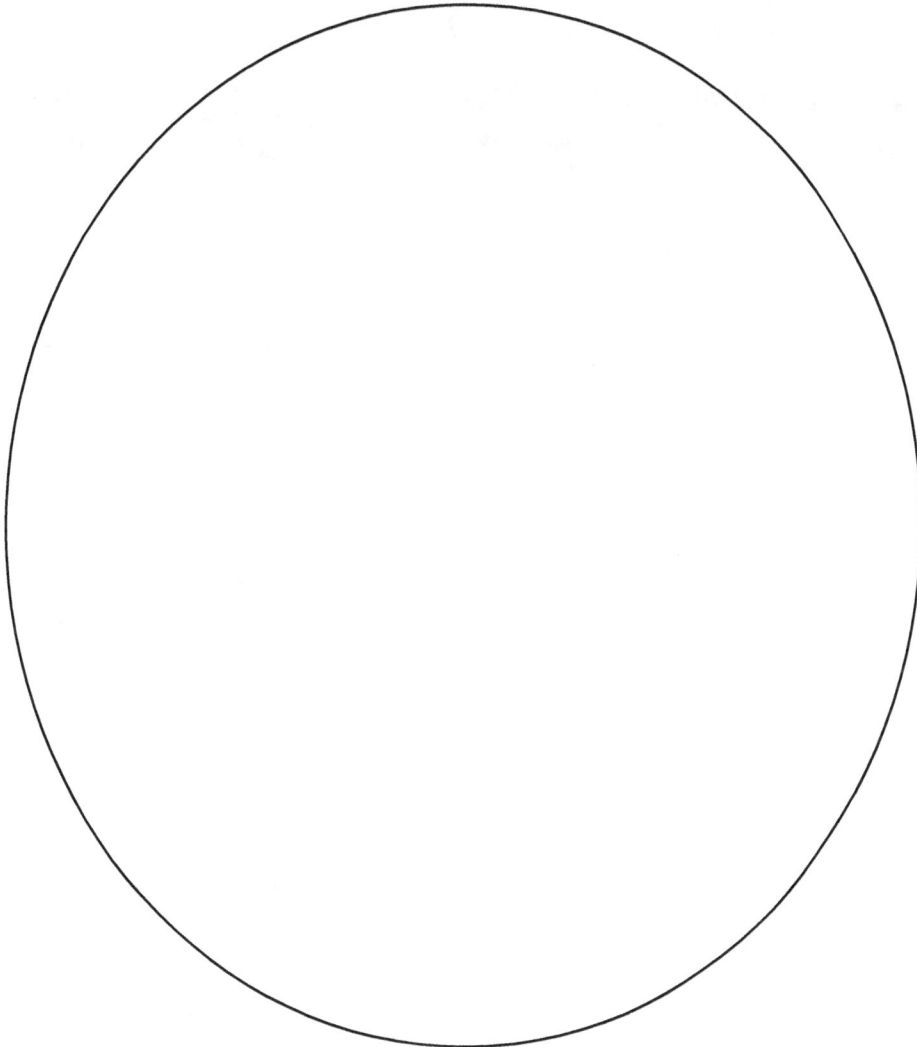

Station 13: Genetics

DOMINANT AND RECESSIVE TRAIT SURVEY

Dominant and Recessive Trait Survey

Trait	Dominant/Recessive	Do you have it?
Freckles	Recessive	
Widow's Peak	Dominant	
Second toe is longer than the first toe	Recessive	
Right-handed	Dominant	
Able to roll your tongue	Dominant	
Cleft chin	Dominant	

Station 14: Your Cells

The Lesson

The slides show cells from humans and plants. Our bodies are made up of billions of specialized cells with specific jobs to do. What our cells do is determined by the genetic code in our DNA, which is found in the nucleus of each cell.

Supplies
▶ 8 handheld microscopes
▶ 14 slides
▶ 8 boxes of colored pencils
▶ Diagram of plant cell
▶ Diagram of animal cell
▶ Copies of the worksheet

Directions for the visitor

1. Push the switch to turn on the handheld microscope.

2. Pick a slide to look at under the microscope.

3. Turn the knob near the power switch until the slide is in focus.

4. What do you see? Compare what you see to the plant or animal cell diagram. Some of the parts are too small for you to see with the handheld microscope, but you might be able to see the nucleus.

5. Draw your observations on the worksheet.

Station 14

YOUR CELLS

Draw what you see under the microscope:

Station 15: Nontoxic Cleaning Products

The Lesson

Many household cleaning products are poisonous and can cause serious health risks. Safe, nontoxic alternatives can be made from simple household products such as lemon juice, vinegar, baking soda, and salt. Some ingredients, such as flour and sugar, do not work.

Supplies

▶ Copies of worksheet

▶ 3 warning labels or empty containers from toxic cleaning products (it helps to enlarge labels on a photocopier)

▶ 1 measuring cup

▶ 1 teaspoon

▶ 1 tablespoon

▶ Mixing bowls (almost any plastic container or large plastic cup will work. It should hold at least 2 cups)

▶ 4 stirring sticks (coffee stirrers work well)

▶ White vinegar

▶ Water

▶ Salt in a small container

▶ Flour in a small container

▶ Sugar in a small container

▶ ¼ cup lemon juice in a small container

▶ Baking soda in a small container

▶ Vegetable oil

▶ Paper towels

Directions for the visitor

1. Look at a cleaning product label and find the warning. Is this product poisonous? At this station you will create a nontoxic cleaner that you can use as an alternative.

2. Look at the ingredients and write down a recipe with the exact amounts of each ingredient.

3. Measure out the exact amounts that you wrote down and pour them into your mixing bowl.

4. Mix the ingredients together with a stirring stick.

5. The volunteer at your station will pour a small amount vegetable oil on the table for you to clean up.

6. Apply your mixture to the oil with a paper towel.

7. What do you observe? Would you change your recipe next time?

Station 15

NONTOXIC CLEANING PRODUCTS

INGREDIENTS	AMOUNT
_____	_____
_____	_____
_____	_____
_____	_____
_____	_____
_____	_____
_____	_____
_____	_____
_____	_____

Children's Hospital Oakland Research Institute

Station 16: Germs Around Us

The Lesson

Invisible microbes are everywhere around us, on everything. When you touch objects, these tiny, invisible organisms get onto your hands. The white powder represents microbes—bacteria, fungi, and viruses—that are on everyday things. Some microbes are harmless and even beneficial, but others are germs that can make us sick. The flu and the common cold are spread by germs. To protect yourself from getting sick, you should wash your hands frequently and always wash them before meals.

Supplies

▶ Lamp, black light (ultraviolet) bulb, and black box

▶ Extension cord

▶ Powder to represent germs
Note: "Germ" powder and black box kits are available from Glo Germ <www.glogerm.com>, Germ Juice <www.germjuice.com>, and GlitterBug (Brevis) <www.brevis.com>

▶ Book: *The Immune System: Your Magic Doctor* (optional)

Household objects sprinkled with "germ" powder:

▶ Crayon or pencil

▶ Cup

▶ Toy

▶ Canned food

▶ Coin

▶ Book

Directions for the visitor

1. Place your hands in the black box and look through the viewing hole.

2. Handle the various household items on the table.

3. Place your hands in the black box and look through the viewing hole again.

4. What do you see? What does the white powder represent?

Station 17: Washing Your Hands

The Lesson

Even if your hands don't look dirty, they are home to billions of bacteria, fungi, and viruses that are waiting to get you sick. People often wash their hands too quickly, without scrubbing the surface and lathering up the soap. To make sure that you get all of the germs, wash your hands for at least 30 seconds, or the time it takes you to sing Happy Birthday twice.

Supplies
- ► 3 bottles of hand sanitizer
- ► 3 stopwatches
- ► Diagrams showing germs on unwashed hands and germs left after 10, 20, and 30 seconds of washing

Directions for the visitor

1. Look at the diagram showing germs on unwashed hands.

2. Take the hand sanitizer bottle and squeeze one dab the size of a penny into your palm.

3. Start the timer and clean your hands for the amount of time that you usually spend washing your hands with soap and water. Stop the timer when you feel that you're done. Remember your time.

4. Turn over the images of hands. The spots represent germs in the areas that the person missed.

5. Find the image that matches the time you spent washing.

6. Are you surprised at the results? What will you try the next time you wash your hands?

Station 17

WASHING YOUR HANDS

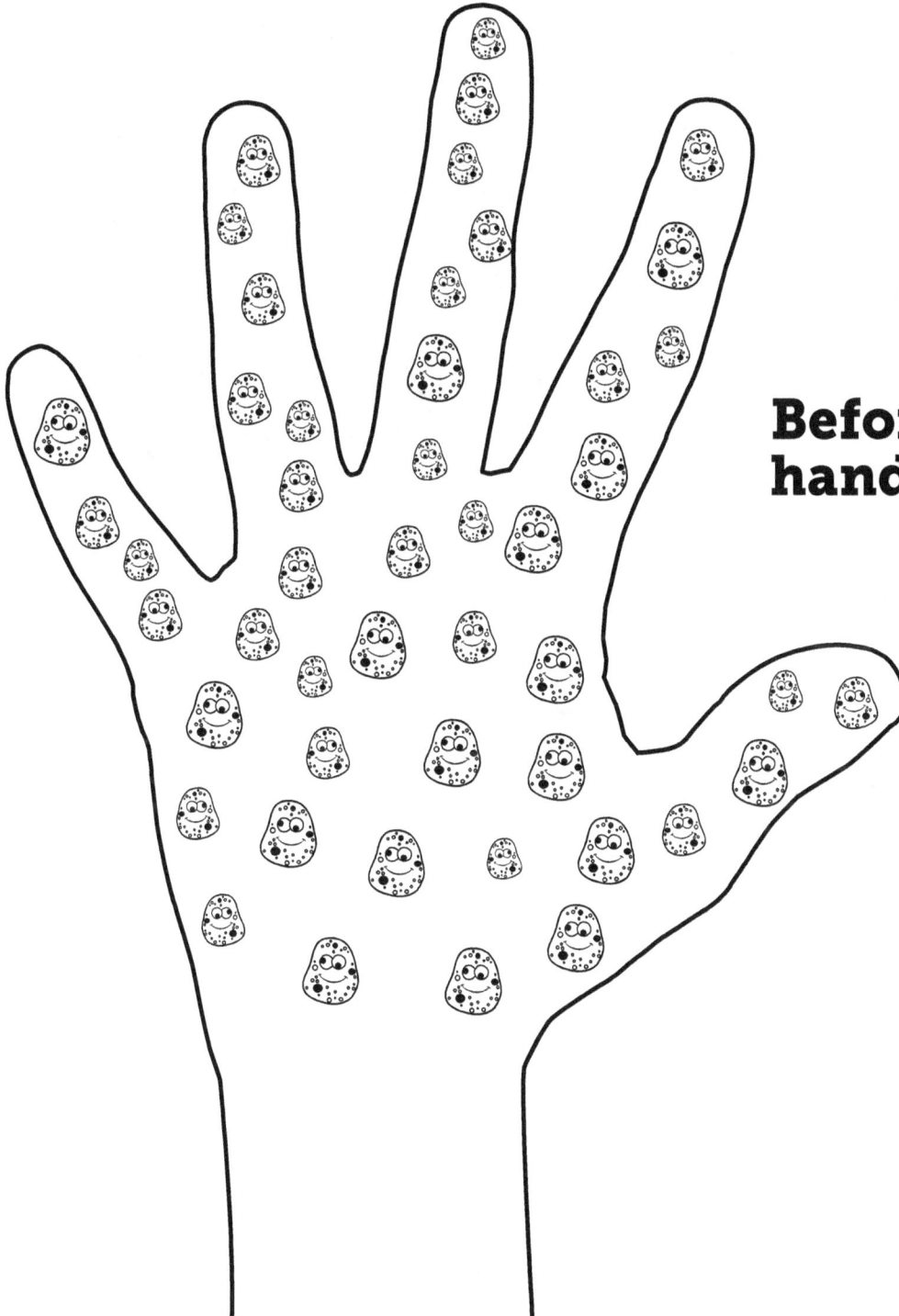

Before handwashing

Station 17

WASHING YOUR HANDS

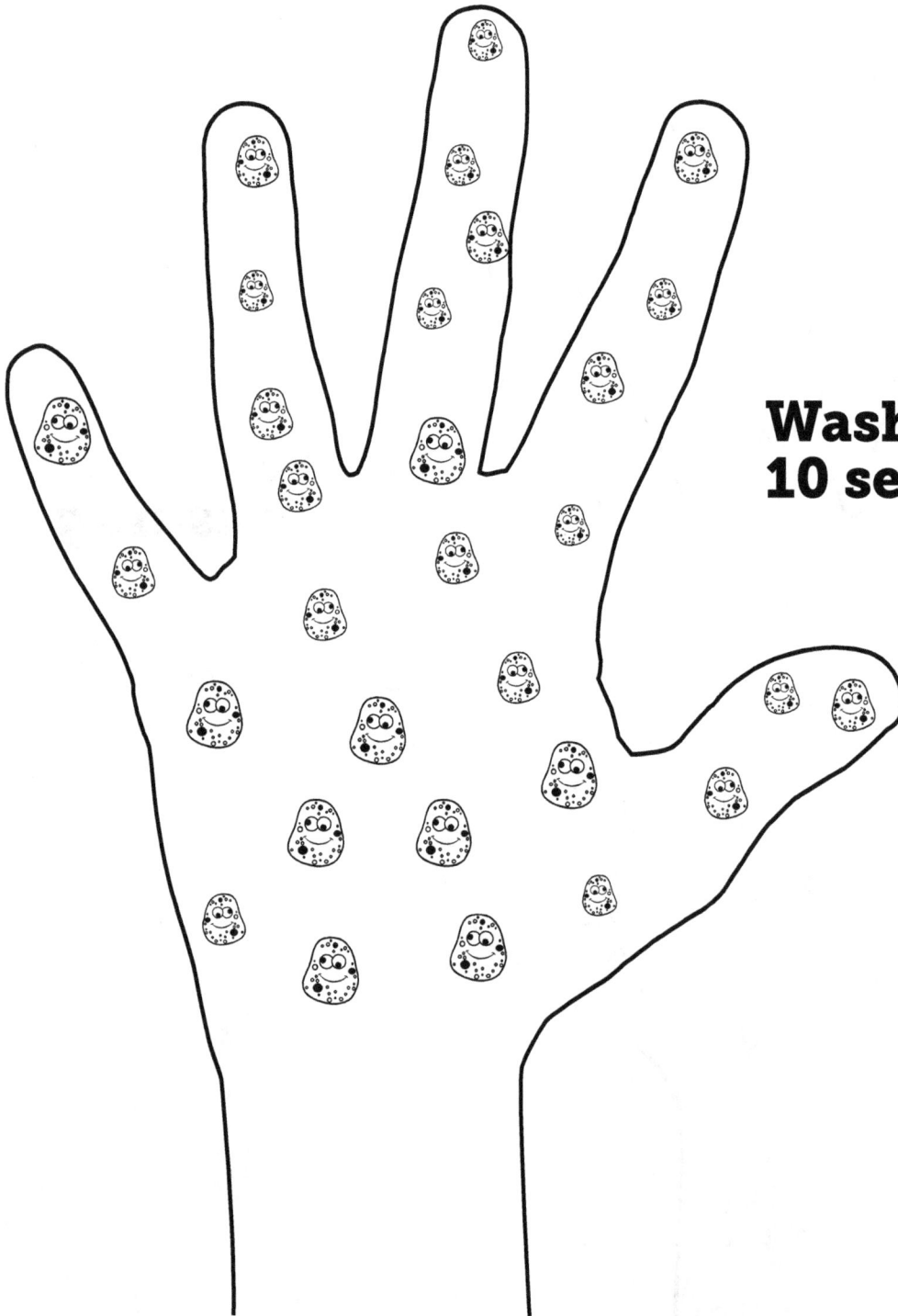

Washing for 10 seconds

Station 17

WASHING YOUR HANDS

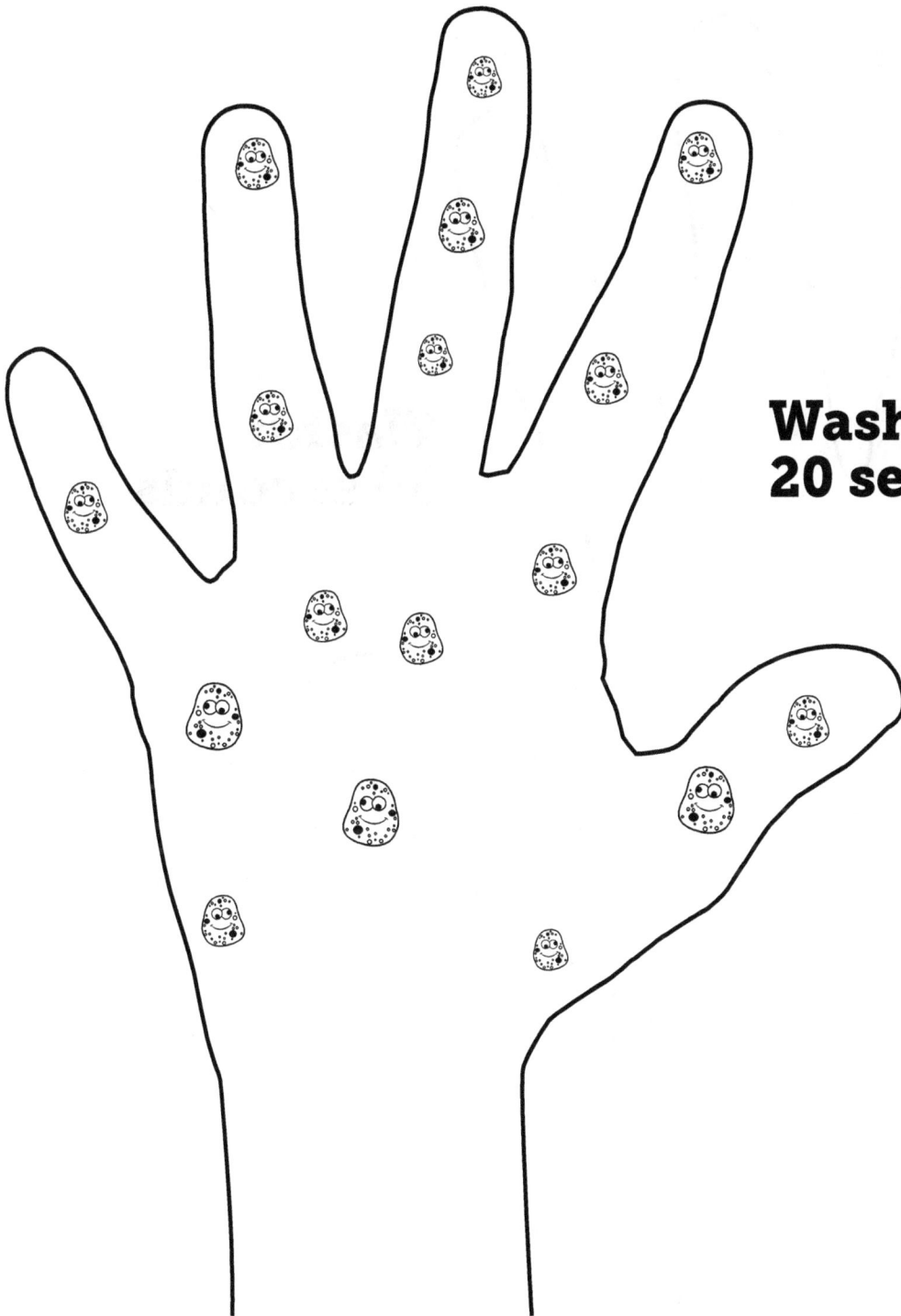

Washing for 20 seconds

Station 17

WASHING YOUR HANDS

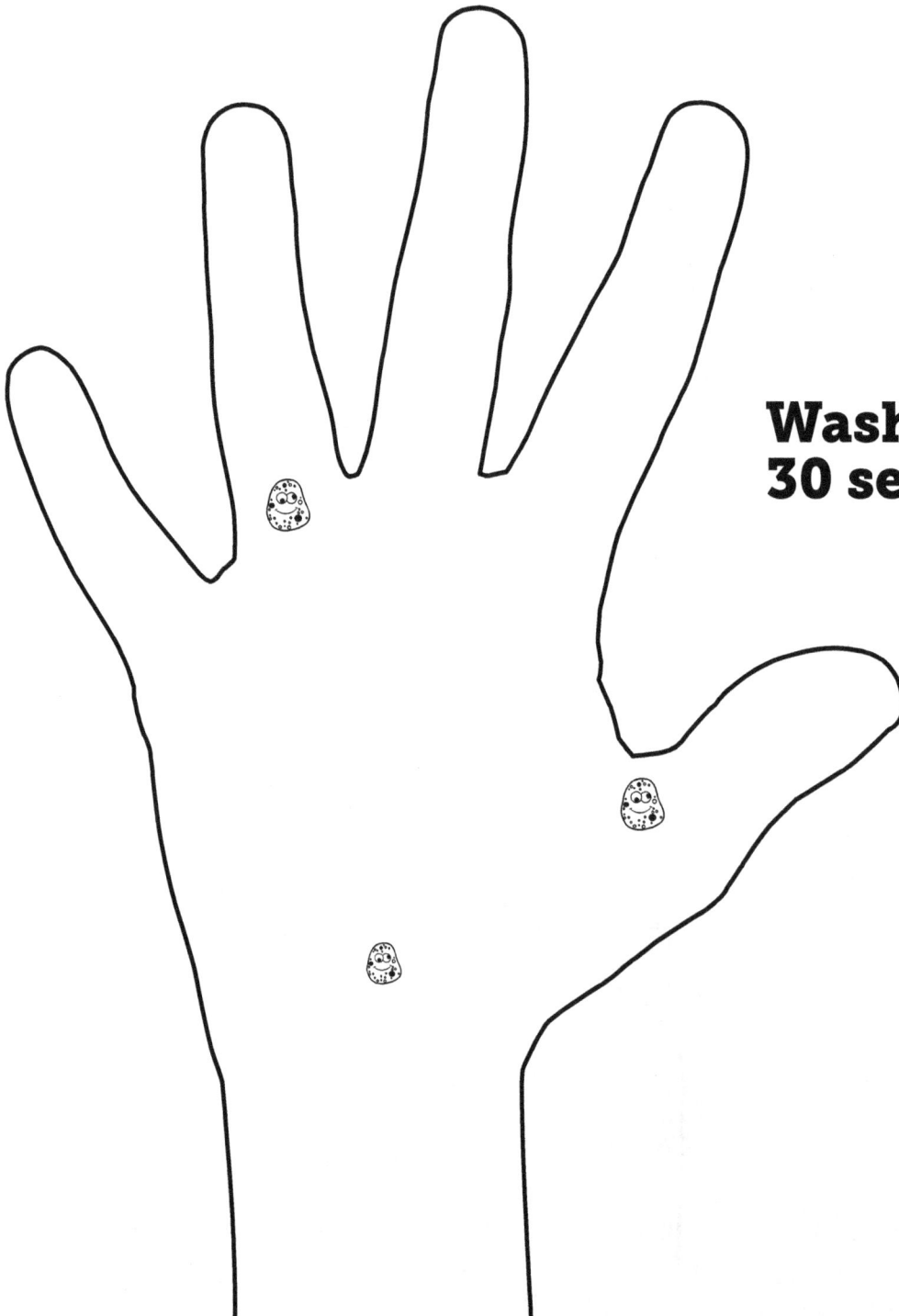

Washing for 30 seconds

Station 18: Healthy Snacks

The Lesson

Many snack foods contain a lot of sugar, salt, and/or fat. Such foods are high in calories and low in nutrients and contribute to tooth decay, diabetes, heart disease, and obesity. Fresh or dried fruits, fresh vegetables, nuts, low-fat yogurt, cheese, and whole grain bread or crackers are all healthier snack choices than sweets, chips, and fried foods.

Supplies

- ▶ Apples, oranges, raisins, grapes, celery, or other healthy snacks
- ▶ Paper towels or napkins
- ▶ Paper plates
- ▶ Garbage bags

Directions for the visitor

- These are examples of healthy snacks that you should be eating.
- Every time you think about grabbing a bag of chips or candy, grab one of these snacks instead!
- Even small choices can make a big difference when it comes to your health.

Station 19: Go Fish

The Lesson

Oceans and bays are polluted with poisons otherwise known as environmental toxics. One common toxic is mercury, a metal naturally found in the earth in very small amounts. Unfortunately, mercury has leaked from mercury mines and other industries into the water, damaging fish and other sea creatures.

- Small creatures absorb mercury and pass it to other fish when they are eaten.
- Larger and older the fish at the top of the food chain contain the most mercury.
- Organisms at the bottom of the food chain contain the least mercury.
- If you regularly eat fish with mercury, you can get poisoned.

Health Effects of Mercury Poisoning (Adults):

- Memory loss
- Tremors
- Shortened attention span
- Vision and hearing loss
- Numbness in fingers and toes
- Kidney damage

Health Effects of Mercury Poisoning (Children):

- Delayed development
- Central nervous system damage
- Urinary and reproductive system damage
- Mental retardation
- Loss of coordination
- Impairment of touch, taste, and sight

What You Can Do:

- Continue to eat fish because it's an excellent source of protein, but try to choose fish low in mercury.
- Avoid eating fish high in mercury, especially if you are pregnant or if you're a child. Limit your consumption to no more than twice a month.
- Avoid eating king mackerel, shark, swordfish, and sturgeon.

Supplies

▶ Fishing pole and line with a clip at the end

▶ 3-sectioned, free-standing poster board painted blue to represent an ocean or bay. Pictures of fish, other sea creatures, and seaweed can be cut out and pasted to the board.

▶ Small pictures of various kinds of fish and other sea plants and animals, such as seaweed, shrimp, crab, mussels, clams, and scallops. Each picture should have from 1 (low) to 4 (high) dots at the bottom to indicate the mercury level (see "Marine Trophic Levels" information sheet to determine number of dots; Level 1 gets 1 dot, Level 2 gets two dots, etc.). A volunteer behind the poster board will clip a picture to the fishing line when the visitor "goes fishing."

▶ A pyramid chart divided into four levels. The bottom level should have 1 dot, the next level 2 dots, the next level 3 dots, and the top level 4 dots to indicate mercury level.

▶ Trophic level information sheet

Directions for the visitor

1. Take the fishing pole and cast the line over the blue board.

2. When you feel a tug, pull the rod out and examine your catch. Then place your catch on the appropriate level of the pyramid chart. The dots indicate how much mercury it contains.

3. Is your catch safe to eat, or should you throw it back? Try catching a few creatures and placing them on the chart. Do you start to see a pattern? What types of fish should you avoid eating?

Station 19

GO FISH

MaRiNe TROphic LeveLS

The organisms at each level eat those at the level below.

LEVEL 4: TERTIARY CONSUMERS

Shark

King mackerel

Marlin

Orange roughy

Rockfish

Swordfish

Tuna

Sturgeon

LEVEL 3: SECONDARY CONSUMERS

Anchovies

Bass

Cod

Halibut

Herring

Salmon

Mahi mahi

Lobster

Shrimp

Crab

Squid

LEVEL 2: PRIMARY CONSUMERS

Mussels

Oysters

Clams

Scallops

Zooplankton (tiny animals that feed on plankton)

LEVEL 1: PRIMARY PRODUCERS

Seaweed

Microscopic algae (phytoplankton), which are actually single-celled plants that come in a wide variety of sizes and shapes

Passport

How to use it

Each visitor to the Festival receives a Passport. At each station, the visitor receives a sticker and writes what he or she learned. After collecting eight stickers, the visitor receives a small prize, such as glow-in-the-dark eyeball or a forehead thermometer strip.

The Passport appears on the next two pages. These pages should be copied back-to-back and folded, so that the finished Passport looks like this:

Front

Back

Activity Station_____		Sticker	Activity Station_____		Sticker
I learned _____			I learned _____		

Inside

YOUR PASSPORT TO THE

Family
Health and
Science Festival

For all students and families

GAMES
ACTIVITIES
FOOD

Learn about:
* Nutrition
* Your Brain
* Your Heart
* Your Lungs...and more!

Collect stickers from activity stations and **win a prize!**

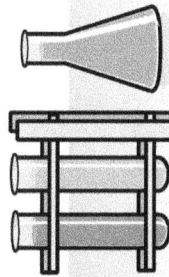

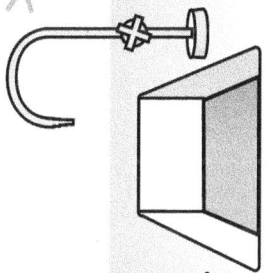

Activity Station _____

I learned _____

Sticker

Activity Station _____

I learned _____

Sticker

Activity Station _____

I learned _____

Sticker

Activity Station _____

I learned _____

Sticker

Activity Station _____

I learned _____

Sticker

Activity Station _____

I learned _____

Sticker

Activity Station _____

I learned _____

Sticker

Activity Station _____

I learned _____

Sticker

www.ingramcontent.com/pod-product-compliance
Lightning Source LLC
Chambersburg PA
CBHW081158090426
42736CB00017B/3383